✪ SPORTS STARS ✪

SCOTTIE PIPPEN

PRINCE OF THE COURT

by Howard Reiser

CHILDRENS PRESS ®

CHICAGO

Picture Acknowledgments

Cover, Focus on Sports; 6, © Bill Smith; 8, 9, AP/Wide World; 11,
© Jeff Carlick/Sports Chrome East/West; 13, AP/Wide World; 14,
UPI/Bettmann; 16 © Bill Smith; 21, AP/Wide World; 23, UPI/Bettmann;
24, © Rich Kane/Sports Chrome East/West; 26, © Bill Smith; 28,
Reuters/Bettmann; 31, UPI/Bettmann; 33, © Bill Smith; 34, 37, AP/Wide
World; 38 ©Bill Smith; 39, Focus on Sports; 41, © Bill Smith; 43, AP/Wide
World; 46, © Bill Smith

Project Editor: Shari Joffe
Design: Beth Herman Design Associates
Photo Editor: Jan Izzo

Acknowledgments

The author would like to thank Tom "Satch" Sanders, vice president of
player programs for the National Basketball Association; Barbara Crockett,
media service assistant for the Chicago Bulls; and the Public Relations
Department of the NBA for their kind assistance in the development of
this biography.

Reiser, Howard.
    Scottie Pippen : prince of the court / by Howard Reiser.
      p. cm.–(Sports stars)
    Summary: A biography of the versatile basketball player who helped
lead the Chicago Bulls to their second straight championship in 1992.
    ISBN 0-516-04366-8
    1. Pippen, Scottie–Juvenile literature. 2. Basketball players–United
States–Biography–Juvenile literature. [1. Pippen, Scottie. 2. Basketball
players. 3. Afro-Americans–Biography.] I. Title. II. Series.
GV884.P55R45   1992
796.323'092–dc20
[B]
                                    92-42023
                                       CIP
                                         AC

SCOTTIE PIPPEN

PRINCE OF THE COURT

He loves ice cream. He loves to clean his cars. He loves the singing voice of Whitney Houston. And he loves to collect record albums. But the one thing he loves most is to play basketball. And fans everywhere love to watch him play.

His name is Scottie Pippen. He plays for the Chicago Bulls of the National Basketball Association. He is considered one of the best all-around players in the league.

Michael Jordan was Scottie's teammate until he retired in 1993. Jordan was the best player in the NBA. Many people thought that Scottie was second-best.

Said former basketball superstar Bill Walton, now a broadcaster, "I consider Scottie the second-best all-around player. The only one who does more is Michael [Jordan]."

Scottie always gives it his all when on the court.

All-time great Bernard King of the Washington Bullets says, "There is nothing Scottie Pippen cannot do. He is a complete player, an all-around great."

Says Chicago Bulls coach Phil Jackson, "Scottie always had great potential. He could shoot. He could play defense. He could pass. He could dribble. He was determined to become a star and to help the Bulls win championships."

Says Satch Sanders, former Boston Celtics great and current NBA vice president of player programs, "Scottie is a superbly gifted player. He has some of the [physical] gifts that Michael Jordan has. He is destined to be a superstar for many years."

Now listen to Michael Jordan: "When Scottie was first drafted in 1987, I had never heard of him. After he joined us, it was obvious he had the ability; that he had immense skills.

"It was just a matter of confidence. All Scottie needed was the confidence that all great players have. He now has that confidence. And he now is a great star."

Scottie is an aggressive, confident player.

Scottie can do it all on the court. He is a point forward who handles the ball as though he were a guard. He makes jump shots, uses his long arms and large hands to help him play great defense, and, with the ball cupped tightly in his right hand, soars over the basket for powerful slam dunks. His trademark is his ability to take the defensive rebound and go the distance— either finishing the play himself, or giving it to teammates. He almost never misses a lay-up in transition.

Scottie is proud of his talent. But he is happiest about two accomplishments: helping lead the Bulls to their third straight championship in 1993, and helping the United States basketball team win a gold medal at the Summer Olympics in Barcelona, Spain.

Scottie was a member of the Dream Team — the gold-medal-winning 1992 U.S. Olympic men's basketball team.

Scottie (wearing tie) was overjoyed when the Bulls brought home their first NBA championship trophy in 1991.

"Winning the NBA championship and then the gold medal were two of my biggest thrills ever," says Scottie. Scottie was overjoyed when the Bulls won their first championship in 1991. But it was even more fun when the Bulls repeated as champs in 1992 and 1993.

"It was a lot easier the first time," says Scottie. "The second time around, everyone is trying to beat you. We had to work very hard to remain on top. Because of that, it was more gratifying to win 1992 than it was the first time." And when the Bulls achieved their amazing "three-peat" in 1993, Scottie realized that he was part of a true sports dynasty.

Scottie smiles more easily than he did when he first joined the Bulls in 1987 as a talented, but unproven, rookie. But even though he is now famous and popular, he still remains a quiet, shy person.

Scottie relaxing at home with his dogs

"Scottie certainly enjoys the life of a celebrity," says a member of the Bulls staff. "But he is basically the same type of person he was when he was younger. He is the same person who sat on the bench while playing high-school ball."

Scottie was born September 25, 1965, in the small town of Hamburg, Arkansas. Scottie was the youngest of twelve children. He had five brothers and six sisters. His father's name was Preston; his mother's, Ethel.

Growing up, Scottie loved sports. He began playing basketball at the age of eleven. As a teenager, he played with his brother and friends for hours at a time at the Pine Street courts.

"Often it was just Scottie and me, just the two of us having fun playing against each other," recalls Ron Martin, a longtime friend. "I was bigger than Scottie. I was able to take advantage of my size."

$\star$ $\star$ $\star$

Scottie made the basketball team at Hamburg High School as a tenth grader. But he spent most games on the bench. Would you be happy if you were not given a chance to play? Well, Scottie was not happy.

Scottie had another reason to be sad. His father, Preston, suffered a stroke that year. It left him paralyzed. He could no longer speak.

Scottie gave thought to quitting basketball. He decided to serve as manager of the football team. This prevented him from working out with the other basketball players during the fall football season. But Scottie enjoyed his football duties too much to give them up.

Basketball coach Donald Wayne was very angry that Scottie had not worked out with the other players. He wanted to throw Scottie off the team. But the other players convinced Wayne to keep Scottie on the team. Unfortunately, Scottie once again spent most of the season on the bench.

Many players would have been discouraged. Not Scottie. As a senior, he returned to the team. He had faith in himself. All he wanted was a chance to play.

Scottie finally got that chance. He became the starting point guard. Now he could impress others with his ability. "Scottie was not a flashy player, but he was good," recalls Wayne. "He was very dependable."

Still, Scottie failed to attract the attention of college coaches. None of them offered him a basketball scholarship or invited him to play at their college. "I was not setting my sights too hard on playing college basketball," recalled Scottie.

Scottie was 6 feet 1½ and weighed only 150 pounds as a high-school senior. But Wayne felt that Scottie could be a good college player. He also felt that it was very important for Scottie to get a college education. Wayne contacted

Don Dyer, the basketball coach at the University of Central Arkansas. Dyer told Wayne that he already had a point guard. But an agreement was worked out for Scottie to receive an education grant to attend the university, and to serve as equipment manager of its basketball team.

Scottie scrimmaged with other players after entering college in the fall of 1983. By now, he was 6 feet 3. Scottie soon made the team. By the end of the season, he was its best player.

Scottie continued to grow and to improve as a player. In his sophomore year, he was 6 feet 5 and weighed 165 pounds. During the season, he averaged nearly 20 points per game. He handled the ball against pressure defense and also played forward and center.

Around this time, Dyer began to feel that Scottie might someday be good enough to play professional basketball. Others agreed, including NBA scouting director Marty Blake.

Scottie was now determined to become a professional. He worked out with weights to make himself stronger. As a junior, he was 6 feet 6, weighed 185 pounds, and made the NAIA All-American team.

He was even bigger and better as a senior. Having grown to 6 feet 7, Scottie averaged 23.6 points and 10 rebounds per game; made nearly 60 percent of his shots, and was selected to the All-American team for the second straight year.

Arch Jones, an assistant coach at Central Arkansas, was an ardent admirer of Scottie's athletic ability. "Even as Scottie continued to grow, he always had great coordination," Jones recalled.

Following his last year in college, Scottie played extremely well at basketball camps. His outstanding performance at the camps drew the attention of professional teams.

On June 22, 1987, Scottie was obtained by the Chicago Bulls in the first round of the draft in a trade with the Seattle SuperSonics. He was the first basketball player from the University of Central Arkansas to reach the pros.

In the first round of the 1987 draft, the Chicago Bulls traded Olden Polynice (left) to the Seattle SuperSonics for Scottie (right).

Scottie is a superb defensive player.

--- ★ ★ ★ ---

"I never thought I would be selected so high in the draft," he admitted. "It was a great feeling."

It was also a great feeling to know he would be a teammate of Michael Jordan's. During practice games in his rookie season, Scottie showed courage and confidence when he volunteered to guard Jordan. This earned him the respect of many. Scottie shrugged off suggestions that Jordan might make him look foolish at practice. "He is not going to do anything against me that he has not done against others," Scottie would answer.

Scottie and teammate Michael Jordan

Some people said it would be easier for Scottie to break into the pros on a team with Jordan than it would be on a team that did not have a superstar. "Everyone will be watching Michael," predicted Al Menendez, director of player personnel of the New Jersey Nets. "They won't be critical of Scottie."

Scottie admitted, however, that playing alongside a superstar could have its disadvantages. "If a player does not get chances to shoot the ball in important situations, it could hurt his confidence and development," said Scottie.

Scottie had a decent rookie season. He averaged nearly 8 points, 3.8 rebounds, and 2.1 assists in fewer than 21 minutes per game. Unfortunately, Scottie needed a back operation after the season. This caused him to miss training camp the following fall, and the first eight games of the 1988-89 season.

In his second season, Scottie finished third in the league in steals.

Scottie played poorly after returning to action. His teammates kidded him when a writer made fun of Scottie's poor play. Scottie's feelings were hurt. He stopped talking to the writer. He then worked hard to become a better player.

"I am going to be an all-star," Scottie promised. Scottie went on to average 14.4 points per game during the season. This was nearly twice as much as he scored in his first season. Scottie also finished third in the league in steals. This proved his great defensive ability.

"Scottie has always loved to play defense," says Bulls general manager Jerry Krause. "He has always had great enthusiasm. He has always had a great attitude. Without it, you cannot excel."

Although Scottie played well during the 1988-89 season, the year ended unhappily for him and the Bulls. Scottie was knocked unconscious early in the sixth game of the Eastern Conference championship against the Detroit Pistons. He never returned to the game. The Bulls lost. Their season was over.

Scottie's dream of becoming an all-star came true during the 1989-90 season. He averaged 16.5 points, 6.7 rebounds, and 5.4 assists per game. The way he soared high in the air and slam-dunked the ball reminded some people of the great "Dr. J." –Julius Erving, Scottie's childhood hero.

But once again, the season ended sadly for Scottie. His father died during the 1990 playoffs. And in the seventh and last game of the Eastern Conference championship, Scottie suffered a migraine headache. He scored only two points as the Bulls lost again to the Pistons.

Scottie sails in for a lay-up.

--- ★ ★ ★ ---

Many fans were angry at Scottie for not helping the Bulls advance further in the playoffs. Some did not believe he had suffered a headache. Others said he did not have courage.

Most players would have been very upset by this reaction. But Scottie was understanding. He agrees that the Bulls might have done better had he played as well as he often had before.

"People don't like excuses," he says. But Scottie admits he was worried after suffering the headache. Scottie was examined by doctors. He was advised to begin wearing eyeglasses to reduce the chance of eye strain. He also decided to take better care of himself.

Scottie made sure he ate breakfast every morning. When he was to play a game at night, he would rest in bed during the afternoon. While resting, he would prepare for the game by thinking about the player he expected to guard.

Studying past games helps Scottie continually improve his performance.

Scottie slam-dunks the ball past Patrick Ewing during the 1991 NBA playoffs.

"I would concentrate on the different moves the player might make," says Scottie. "I felt this would help me get ready for the game and become a better player."

It certainly did not hurt. The 1990-91 season was a great one for Scottie and the Bulls. Scottie averaged a career-high 17.8 points and 7.3 rebounds per game in the regular season. He played even better in the playoffs, helping lead the Bulls to their first world championship.

Scottie kissed the championship trophy during the Bulls celebration. He was bursting with pride. He had finally proven that he could play like a star in important games.

No one was happier than Michael Jordan, his superstar teammate. Jordan reminded writers that they had questioned Scottie's courage in the past. "Scottie's got a lot a pride," Jordan said.

"He was out to prove something. He was determined to be a force." Scottie continued to excel during the 1991-92 season. He made the all-star team for the second time. He also averaged career highs of 21 points and 7.7 rebounds per game.

And once again, Scottie helped spark the Bulls to another championship. He averaged 19.5 points and nearly 9 rebounds per game in the playoffs, while earning praise for his leadership and ball-handling talent.

Scottie played a major role in the Bull's success during the 1991-92 season.

Scottie helped lead the Bulls to victory in the 1992 NBA Finals.

Scottie shone in the sixth game of the Eastern Conference Finals, when the Bulls put away the Cleveland Cavaliers. Then, in the sixth and decisive game of the NBA Finals against the Portland Trail Blazers, Scottie helped lead the Bulls to a spectacular come-from-behind victory after the team was trailing by 15 points in the fourth quarter.

Scottie hugs the Chicago Bulls' second-straight NBA Championship trophy in 1992.

In 1993, Scottie again helped lead the Bulls
to an NBA championship. This made the Bulls
the first team since the 1960s to win three
straight championships.

Michael Jordan decided to retire before the
next season began. He said he had accomplished
everything he could in professional basketball.
In training camp in October 1993, Scottie moved
into Michael's old locker. Now it was Scottie's
turn to lead the Bulls. He was now their best
player, and maybe the best player in the league.

Scottie has come a long way from his boyhood
days in Hamburg, Arkansas. Most importantly,
he now has a lot of faith in himself. "It is very
important to have confidence," Scottie says.
"My main strength is the confidence that I have
in my all-around ability."

Off the court, he takes great pride in taking
care of his cars. "I clean my cars very well,"
he boasts. "I have a lot of cleaning supplies
in my garage."

Scottie and teammate Horace Grant are close friends.

★ ★ ★

Scottie says it is important to be kind.
He says that someday you may want someone
to be kind to you. Scottie is divorced, and
has a young son. He says parents should teach
their children that drugs are very bad. "Drugs
can ruin your life," Scottie warns. "Drugs can
kill you."

Scottie and teammate Horace Grant are
close friends. The Bulls once asked each player
to name the person he would invite on a trip to
the moon. The answer would be printed in the
Bulls yearbook.

"Horace Grant," Scottie answered.

Players on other teams would love Scottie
to take a trip to the moon. Especially during
the basketball season.

Then they would not have to worry about
playing against the man hailed as one of the
best basketball players in the world.

Chronology

1965 – Scottie Pippen is born in Hamburg, Arkansas, on September 25, the son of Preston and Ethel Pippen.

1976 – Scottie begins playing basketball at the age of eleven.

1980 – As a tenth grader, Scottie makes the Hamburg High School basketball team. He sits on the bench most of the season.

1981 – Scottie decides to serve as manager of the football team. This prevents him from joining other basketball players in pre-season workouts.
   – Scottie is on the basketball team for the second straight year. Once again, he sits on bench most of the time.

1982 – Scottie wins the position of starting point guard on the basketball team. He has a fine season.

1983 – Scottie enrolls at the University of Central Arkansas on an education grant. He serves as manager of the basketball team. He later makes the team as a player.

1985 – Scottie averages 18.5 points per game in his sophomore year.

1986 – As a junior, Scottie averages 19.8 points and 9.2 rebounds per game, and is selected an NAIA All-American.

1987 – Now 6 feet 7 inches tall, Scottie averages 23.6 points and 10 rebounds per game and makes the All-American team for the second straight year.
 – Scottie is obtained by the Chicago Bulls in the first round of the draft through a trade with Seattle.

1989 – Scottie averages 14.4 points per game during the regular season. He also plays great defense.

1990 – Scottie averages 16.5 points per game.
 – He is named to the NBA All-Star Team for the first time.

1991 – Scottie averages 17.8 points per game during the regular season and 21.6 points per game in the playoffs as the Bulls win the NBA Championship.
 – Showing his all-around talent, Scottie is named to the NBA All-Defensive Second Team.

1992 – Scottie averages 21 points and 7.7 rebounds per game during the regular season and 19.5 points per game during the playoffs as the Bulls win their second straight championship.

– Scottie is named to the NBA All-Star Team for the second time. He also is chosen to the NBA All League Second Team and to the NBA All-Defensive First Team.

– Scottie takes part in the 1992 Summer Olympic Games in Barcelona, Spain, as a member of the gold-medal-winning U.S. men's basketball team; this "Dream Team," touted as the best basketball team ever assembled, included such NBA superstars as Michael Jordan, Magic Johnson, Larry Bird, and Charles Barkley.

1993 – Scottie is the Bulls' second-leading scorer for the fourth year in a row, averaging 18.6 points and 7.7 rebounds per game. He is named to the NBA All-Defensive First Team and helps lead the Bulls to their third straight championship.

⋆ ⋆ ⋆

About the Author

Howard Reiser has been a well-known New York City newspaper reporter, columnist, and bureau chief. He has also worked as a labor news writer and editor. Today a political speechwriter, Mr. Reiser covered the major news stories in New York City for more than twenty-five years.

Mr. Reiser is the author of several other books for young people, including *Jackie Robinson, Baseball Pioneer.* He and his wife, Adrienne, live in New York. They have four children: Philip, Helene, Steven, and Stuart.